FUN WITH PEANUTS

FUN WITH

Selected Cartoons from
GOOD OL' CHARLIE BROWN
(Volume 1)

PEANUTS®

by Charles M. Schulz

A FAWCETT CREST BOOK

FAWCETT PUBLICATIONS, INC., GREENWICH, CONN.
MEMBER OF AMERICAN BOOK PUBLISHERS COUNCIL, INC.

FUN WITH PEANUTS

This book, prepared especially for Fawcett Publications, Inc., comprises the first half of GOOD OL' CHARLIE BROWN, and is reprinted by arrangement with Holt, Rinehart and Winston, Inc.

Tenth Fawcett Crest printing, July 1967

Published by Fawcett World Library,
67 West 44th Street, New York, New York 10036.
Printed in the United States of America.

SCHULZ

I NEVER REALIZED THE TROUBLES THAT A BASEBALL MANAGER HAS.. EVERYBODY COMES TO HIM WITH THEIR PROBLEMS...

HEY, MANAGER... TIE MY SHOE!

SURE

GET OUT OF HERE!!

SCHULZ

OH, YES, SO HE IS..

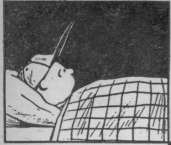

MONDAY IS OUR FIRST GAME, AND I'M SCARED TO DEATH..

WHAT A TEAM I'VE GOT... FIVE BOYS, THREE GIRLS AND A DOG! GOOD GRIEF!!

I DON'T KNOW WHY I EVER TRIED TO BE A MANAGER..I MUST BE OUT OF MY MIND!

I WONDER IF CASEY STENGEL IS ASLEEP?

SCHULZ

TWANG!

RATS!

WHOP

WHAT ARE YOU TRYIN' TO DO, **KILL SOMEBODY?**

WHEN AUTUMN IS OVER, LINUS, WINTER COMES

AND WHEN WINTER COMES, WE CAN THROW SNOWBALLS AND MAKE SNOWMEN! WON'T THAT BE FUN?

Boy! I'LL SAY!

I WONDER WHAT 'SNOW' IS?

SCHULZ

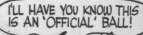

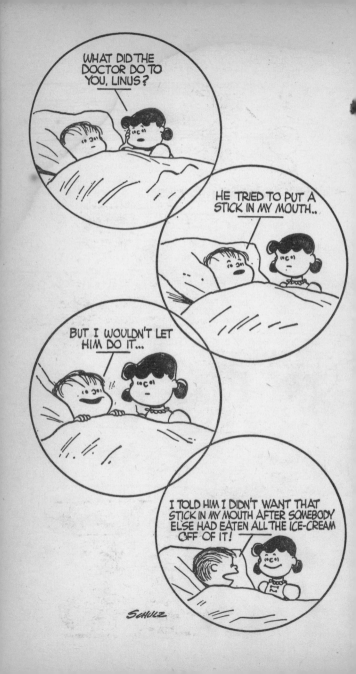

"Jack fell down, and broke his crown, and Jill came tumbling after."

MAY I USE ONE OF YOUR PENCILS, CHARLIE BROWN?

THANK YOU..

I ALWAYS LIKE TO UNDERLINE PARTICULARLY SIGNIFICANT PASSAGES..

SCHULZ

MOM! I'M COMING IN NOW...

WHY DON'T YOU STAY OUTSIDE, AND PLAY?

WELL...

THERE WAS THIS CATERPILLAR ON THE SIDEWALK... AND HE WAS CRAWLING RIGHT AT ME...

SO I FIGURED I MIGHT AS WELL COME IN, AN' WATCH T.V.

SCHULZ

LISTEN TO THIS, SCHROEDER..

"A NEW BEETHOVEN HALL IS BEING BUILT ON THE BANKS OF THE RHINE RIVER.."

"THE MODERN STONE STRUCTURE WILL COST OVER A MILLION DOLLARS"

SPARE NO EXPENSE!!!!!

SCHULZ

SIX CENTS! I KNOCK ON EVERY DOOR IN THE NEIGHBORHOOD, AND WHAT DO I GET? SIX CENTS!

TOSS THAT PENNY IN THE AIR, AND I'LL SHOW YOU SOMETHING..
O.K.... SHOW ME SOMETHING...
BANG!
FASTEST GUN IN THE WEST!
SCHULZ

SCHULZ

Billy and Susie are twins. They live in the city.

Here is their house. It is white. Here is their car. It is red.

In the morning Father goes to work. Mother cleans the house. The children play in the yard.

HERE'S A BOOK I THINK MAYBE YOU'LL LIKE, CHARLIE BROWN... IT GIVES A FASCINATING DESCRIPTION OF LIFE IN THE CITY!

SCHULZ

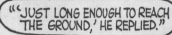

I THOUGHT I TOLD YOU TO STOP THAT DANCING?! YOU HAVE NO RIGHT TO BE SO HAPPY!!! NOW, STOP IT! DO YOU HEAR ME?!

SCHULZ

ANOTHER FEW WEEKS AND ALL THE BIRDS WILL BE COMING BACK...

COMING BACK? COMING BACK FROM WHERE?

FROM THE SOUTH.. DIDN'T YOU KNOW THAT BIRDS FLY SOUTH FOR THE WINTER?

HA HA HAHAHAHA

IN ALL MY LIFE, CHARLIE BROWN, I'VE NEVER KNOWN ANYONE WITH AN IMAGINATION LIKE YOURS!

SCHULZ

I'VE BEEN WATCHING THESE BUGS, CHARLIE BROWN...

YOU SEE, THIS ONE BUG HERE IS ABOUT TO LEAVE HOME...HE'S BEEN SAYING GOOD-BYE TO ALL HIS FRIENDS

SUDDENLY THIS LITTLE GIRL BUG COMES RUNNING UP, AND TRIES TO PERSUADE HIM NOT TO LEAVE...

IF YOU'RE GOING TO BE A GOOD 'BUG-WATCHER', YOU HAVE TO HAVE LOTS OF IMAGINATION!

SCHULZ